The Big Book for Our Planet

Edited by Ann Durell, Jean Craighead George,
and Katherine Paterson

Designed by Jane Byers Bierhorst

•

Dutton Children's Books NEW YORK

THE BIG BOOK FOR OUR
PLANET

WRITTEN BY

Aliki / Jim Arnosky / Natalie Babbitt / John Bierhorst
Lynne Cherry / Pam Conrad / Tomie dePaola
Jean Craighead George / Ruth Heller / Tana Hoban
H. M. Hoover / X. J. Kennedy / Karla Kuskin
Myra Cohn Livingston / Lois Lowry
Patricia MacLachlan / David McPhail / Milton Meltzer
Jack Prelutsky / Laurence Pringle / Anne Rockwell
Joanne Ryder / Marilyn Sachs / Seymour Simon
William Sleator / Stephanie S. Tolan
Rosemary Wells / Jane Yolen

ILLUSTRATED BY

Aliki / Jim Arnosky / Quentin Blake / Lynne Cherry
Kay Chorao / Barbara Cooney / Tomie dePaola
Leo and Diane Dillon / Debra Frasier / Diane Goode
Ruth Heller / Tana Hoban / Susan Jeffers
Steve Johnson and Lou Fancher / Steven Kellogg
David McPhail / Tracey Campbell Pearson
Jerry Pinkney / Ted Rand / Anne Rockwell
Seymour Simon / Merlin D. Tuttle
Chris Van Allsburg / Wendy Watson
Rosemary Wells / Paul O. Zelinsky

Published in the United States 1993 by Dutton Children's Books,
a division of Penguin Books USA Inc.
375 Hudson Street, New York, New York 10014

Printed in U.S.A.
First edition
1 3 5 7 9 10 8 6 4 2

Library of Congress Cataloging-in-Publication Data

The big book for our planet
Ann Durell, Jean Craighead George, Katherine Paterson, editors.—1st ed.
p.   cm.
Summary • Nearly thirty stories, poems, and nonfiction pieces by such
notable authors as Natalie Babbitt, Marilyn Sachs, and Jane Yolen,
illustrated by the likes of Paul O. Zelinsky and Chris Van Allsburg,
demonstrate some of the environmental problems now plaguing our planet,
including overpopulation, tampering with nature,
litter, pollution, and waste disposal.
ISBN 0-525-45119-6
1. Environmental protection—Literary collections.
2. Children's literature, American.
[1. Environmental protection—Literary collections.]
I. Durell, Ann.   II. George, Jean Craighead.   III. Paterson, Katherine.
PZ5.B438   1993   [Fic]—dc20   92-33433   CIP
AC

Title page illustration by David McPhail

INTRODUCTION

Hold this book in your hands and sit down. Sit on the floor, a sofa, a street curb, or in a wooded park under a tree.

It is time to think about our planet.

Think about this: As far as we know, the Earth is the only planet in the universe on which there is life.

Then think about this: Once we human beings shared the grasslands of Africa with lions and springbok and elephants. We saw more bison on the plains of North America than people. We lived in the rain forest with millions of species. We permitted Asia's water buffalo, hawks, and eagles to go their way because we respected all life.

We marveled at the other inhabitants of our planet. Some could live inside a leaf, others thrived in a hot spring or on the polar ice cap. We wondered and learned from them.

Meanwhile we thought the forests and the seas were endless. But today, at the end of the twentieth century, we know they are not.

Now open *The Big Book for Our Planet*. The poems, stories, and articles have been written and illustrated by authors and artists who say that what the Earth needs is more clean water, fresh air, trees, bats, whales, and mushrooms—and less garbage, traffic, and pollution.

This book says we can work with our planet, not against it.

The editors wish to offer thanks on behalf of the Earth to all the artists and authors who have filled this book so wonderfully and also to Bruce Brooks, Jennifer Dewey, and Patricia Lauber.

Ann Durell, Jean Craighead George, Katherine Paterson
Coeditors

Contents

The Big Book for Our Planet

Oh World, I Wish

·

BY *Jane Yolen*

·

ILLUSTRATED BY *Susan Jeffers*

Oh World, I wish you were my mother,
For I would spread my fingers out
Against your earth face
And smell again the good brown smell.
I would feel your body warm by mine,
More than sun and fire and coals.
I would taste your silky streams
And the cold clean waters

Running over twenty-one stones.
I would lift my face to your sky.

Oh World, I wish you were my father,
For I would burrow into your marshes
And twine your green fingers in mine.
I would feel my face against yours,
Woody and barkish and rough.
And I would touch the slippery stones
As soft as tears and as shiny.
Your gray boulders, like muscles,
Would bunch up against my back.
I would lift my face to your sky.

Oh World, I wish you were my brothers,
I wish you were my sisters,
For we would play in the long grass
And the wind would swing it like hair:
Swee-swash, swee-swash.
We would make combs of acacia and thorn

And plait feathers in our braids.
I would share my bowl with you,
And you would share yours with me.
I would lift my face to your sky.

Oh World, I wish we were a family
Of flesh and earth and stone.
Oh World, I wish we were a family
Of blood and sand and bone.

Take Time

•

B Y *Tana Hoban*

We live in an incredible world.

Take time to look and take notice.

Take time to look closely and carefully.

Take time to care.

The Last Days of the Giddywit

·

BY *Natalie Babbitt*

·

ILLUSTRATED BY *Steven Kellogg*

Years and years ago, in the time when houses were caves—this was after the dinosaurs but a while before shovels—there was a tribe of people called the Giddywit. They lived all together, and every day the men would go out and hunt supper while the women stayed home to

A Giddywit battling a fly.

THE PREHISTORIC MUSEUM

pick nuts and berries and teach the babies how to swat flies. Then at night, when the men came back, everyone would feast on mammoth meat or reindeer, with a side of the nuts and berries, and they tossed the garbage in a corner.

After a few weeks, of course, the pile of garbage would get pretty big and smelly, and the flies were something fierce, so the Giddywit would pack up their furs and clubs, and the babies' bibs and swatters, and move to a new cave. This always caused great confusion, with snarling and arguments, and once in a while a baby would get left behind and have to be fetched. But soon the Giddywit would be settled again in a nice fresh place and could start over, tossing garbage and swatting flies.

Now, there was among the Giddywit a thin little man named Oog who wasn't allowed to hunt mammoths because he only got in the way. So his job was to look for eggs. He was good at climbing trees, way up where the nests were, and while he was up there, he would look out over the land where everything was wild and sweet and didn't ever seem to get smelly. "This is nice," he would say to himself. "I wish *we* could live in trees." But they couldn't because of having to hang on, even while sound asleep, which would have been hard for everyone, especially the babies. Still, Oog thought a lot about how nice it was, far away from the garbage.

One night in the cave—it was summer, and the flies and the garbage were atrocious—Oog said to everyone, "Why don't we try putting the garbage outside?"

"Outside?" said everyone. "You're a dope, Oog. If you want to bring every bear and tiger in the neighborhood nosing around the door, that's the way to do it." And they snickered at Oog and poked each other with their elbows and winked.

"We could dig holes and bury the garbage, maybe," said Oog.

"Who's got time to dig holes?" they said, with more snickers and winks. "Sure, if we had a shovel. But it's still a while before shovels. And anyway, what's wrong with moving to a new cave?"

"We might run out of caves," said Oog.

"Run out of caves!" they cried. "You're a dope, Oog." And they winked and poked each other again and threw more garbage in a corner, and then they lay down on their furs and went to sleep.

But Oog sat up, swatting flies, and thought it over. And the next morning, instead of climbing trees to look for eggs, he took Mrs. Oog by the hand and went away, a long way off, miles and miles through the wild, sweet land, and came after many days to a little cave just right for two. "This is the ticket," he said to Mrs. Oog. "We'll live on nuts and berries and the very occasional rabbit, and of

Oog Dreaming

course we'll always have eggs. And we'll never throw garbage into corners."

"But, dear," said Mrs. Oog, "what will we *do* with the garbage? We'll have to put it *some*where."

"We'll bury it," said Oog.

"But, dear," said Mrs. Oog, "we can't do that without shovels to dig the holes."

"We won't need very big holes," said Oog. "Not with only two. So I shall invent the spoon and dig with that."

"Clever," said Mrs. Oog. "And I shall invent the fork. To keep our fingers clean at supper. It's time."

So Oog and Mrs. Oog invented the spoon and fork and buried their garbage outside the cave, and everything stayed nice and clean, and they were happy as clams even though they'd never seen a clam, until one day, a year or so later, here came the rest of the Giddywit, tramping along with their furs and babies, arguing and snarling.

"Well, well," said Oog. "What brings the lot of you to *these* far parts?"

"We ran out of caves," said everyone. "And now you're going to snicker, aren't you?"

"No," said Oog, "but maybe you've learned that you have to bury your garbage."

"Can't do it," said everyone. "It's still too long before shovels."

"Maybe so," said Oog, "but I've invented the spoon, which is pretty good for digging."

"Oog," they said, "you're still a dope. Digging with a—what did you call it? A spoon?—is too much work for the kind of hole *we'd* need. We'll just go on and look for another bunch of caves."

So they did, still snarling and arguing, and Oog never saw them again, except, as it happens, for the babies. For the Giddywit found a new cave farther on and settled down to tossing and swatting. And then one night, when the wind was in the right direction, some bears and tigers sniffed out the cave and finished off the Giddywit, except for the babies, and left no garbage at all. The babies found their way back to Oog and Mrs. Oog, who, having no babies of their own, were delighted. And Oog made a great big spoon to dig holes with, so that shovels were invented at last, because what is a shovel but a great big spoon?

So that was the end of the Giddywit and the start of the Oogites, a neat and tidy tribe from which we are all descended.

Mr. and Mrs. Oog teaching the baby Giddywits.

Maybe.

The Mushroom

·

BY *H. M. Hoover*

In A.D. 450 a squirrel could travel from the east coast of North America to the Mississippi without ever leaving the trees.

That year a squirrel, while grooming, brushed several million mushroom spores from its fur.

So small that a hundred million could fit into a teaspoon, the spores floated. Some rose up into the atmosphere; some were carried around the world by the jet stream. Most drifted to the forest floor.

There was a massive, rolling earthquake, followed by electrical storms. Rain fell lightly, steadily, for days.

From two of those spores a new mushroom began to grow. It sent out microscopic filaments, called hyphae, to penetrate and feed on forest debris. A sheath of a thousand hyphae is no thicker than a human hair.

The hyphae secreted enzymes to break down complex carbohydrates into sugars on which the mushroom fed. Needing protein for a balanced diet, the fungi filaments hunted, entrapping and digesting amoebas, bacteria, and tiny worms.

Within months miles of hyphae twisted through the forest floor. The fungi fruited, producing a new mushroom.

A chipmunk and several beetles ate most of the mushroom, scattering spores. Soon a ring-shaped colony of mushrooms marked the spot where the parent once stood.

In Europe, Attila the Hun died in 453. Tea was brought to China from India.

The ancient forest remained undisturbed. Rains fell and summer nights were warm. Within a few years the mushroom's filaments had spread through an acre and weighed two thousand five hundred pounds.

By the time Arthur, king of the Britons, died in 537, the mushroom had consumed almost a century of fallen trees. Its filaments stretched through ten acres of the forest floor, fruiting in circles the Britons would have called fairy rings.

That year the plague reached northern Europe. A third of the population died. Earthquakes shook the entire world. The Byzantine Empire began to crumble.

The mushroom went on growing.

By 750 the Venerable Bede had written his history of England, newspapers were being printed in China, and some Europeans slept in beds instead of on the floor.

The mushroom's total weight now exceeded eighteen tons, all of it hidden beneath the surface of the forest floor.

By the year 1000, in North America, the Mississippian people lived in handsome cities, but the pueblos of Mesa Verde were running short of water. In the century to come humans sometimes walked over the mushroom's growth. Their moccasins left no footprints.

About that time white men first walked among the tall trees. Fierce as they were, the ancient forest frightened them. It was too big, too dark, too endless. They spent a night in the shelter of a giant hollow oak. When morning came, they hurried back to their Viking ship and fled. They left their fire burning. The tree, mortally wounded, fell in an autumn storm.

The mushroom's hyphae sought out the fallen tree

and began to return its mass to the earth and air. Seedlings rooted in the damp, rotting bark.

By 1066 a colonnade of tall trees grew over the giant log, embracing it with their buttress roots. In Europe, Westminster Abbey was consecrated, York Cathedral begun, Edward the Confessor died horribly, his successor was killed in the Battle of Hastings. Then, too, an Italian monk taught his brother monks to sing *do, re, mi,* and the comet later called Halley's appeared. Again.

The comet was as indifferent as the forest and the mushroom to the affairs of humankind.

The Crusades came and went. Saladin terrified all infidels. The Chinese introduced tea to their neighbors, the Japanese. Marco Polo, against his will, was given time to dictate his memoirs. Queens were still the only women noted by historians.

The mushroom's hyphae now spread through more than thirty acres; its mass exceeded thirty-eight tons. It had lived nearly a thousand years when Joan of Arc was burned at the stake. The Incas had begun to rule Peru. Lorenzo de' Medici and Christopher Columbus were born. The book-publishing profession began.

In 1592, in Holland, windmills were first used to power mechanical saws.

The day the Pilgrims landed at New Plymouth, the end of the ancient forest became only a matter of time—

a long time in human terms, but not for the forest, or the mushroom.

The mushroom's filaments had woven through more than two hundred acres. The weight of its total mass was now as unimaginable as the infinite smallness of the two original spores had once been.

Europeans had no more than landed when they began to cut down trees. Forests that had been evolving for ten thousand years into perfect ecosystems disappeared in two centuries.

The mushroom's home, far from the coast, survived longer than most. Inexorably the settlers came, cutting, burning, blasting, plowing around the stumps.

In the winter of 1866 the mushroom's forest was cut, the wood sold to the Union army. The frozen soil saved the mushroom from destruction. Seedlings sprouted in the sunlight of the following spring. Deer grazed among the fairy rings.

In 1904 a German couple bought the land where the mushroom grew. Father and sons slowly cleared the trees and plowed, and replowed. Only forty acres were spared as "woods."

In 1984 the family farm was sold to a developer. Bulldozers arrived. A shopping mall was built over the rich fields. A parking lot covered the acres that had long been forest. Sun on the black asphalt superheated the earth below.

The week before the mall's opening, rain fell softly, steadily, for days. One night a bulge appeared on the surface of the parking lot, and another and another. Soon there were too many to count, and they formed circular patterns.

Had you been there, you might have heard above the rain the rasp of breaking asphalt, the slow cracking of masonry walls, cascades of breaking glass.

Morning light revealed that the mall and parking lot had been lifted and were being held aloft atop the caps of millions of mushrooms . . . fairy rings.

As the mushrooms aged, the buildings standing on them swayed and sagged. Girders detached, roofs fell in, walls collapsed. In the parking lot the light poles stood at crazy angles, creaking in the wind that blew across a field of broken asphalt.

By noon the mushrooms had released trillions of spores to the wind. Some spores rose into the atmosphere to travel with the jet stream. Others drifted into the wreckage or were washed into raw earth.

New mushrooms began to grow. They sent out microscopic filaments to penetrate and feed upon the debris. A sheath of a thousand hyphae is no thicker than a human hair.

Little Whale and Jonah

·

BY *Marilyn Sachs*

·

ILLUSTRATED BY *Tracey Campbell Pearson*

Father Whale worried about the planet.

He worried about pollution and junk food and, most especially, he worried about endangered species.

"Just look," he told a gathering of the PWP (Parent Whales of the Planet), "at what happened to the dinosaurs, the dodo bird, and the moa. It wasn't their fault that they became extinct, but now we have another creature to worry about. It's called Human, and it is pitiful, helpless, foolish, and self-destructive."

"But Humans are multiplying alarmingly," said one of the mothers. "They are crowding out more benevolent inhabitants of this planet and generally making pests of themselves."

"That is true," said Father Whale. "Which only shows how foolish and self-destructive they are. Because if they keep on going the way they have been, they will certainly become extinct."

"They hunt our brothers and sisters," said another father. "I say good riddance to them, if they really are on their way out. They've done nothing but cause trouble for the rest of us."

"No, no, no!" Father Whale insisted. "We must preserve all the creatures on this planet, although"—here Father Whale shook his head sadly—"some are less lovable than others."

Father Whale tried to make sure that Little Whale understood what was right. "Look out for others," Father Whale told him. "Keep your eyes open all the time. Keep your mouth closed. And don't eat junk food."

But Little Whale didn't always do what his father told him.

(Jonah didn't always do what he was told either.)

One day Little Whale came home from school with a bellyache.

"I have a bellyache," he told Father Whale.

"Did you keep your eyes open and your mouth closed?" Father Whale asked.

"Oh," said Little Whale. "I thought you said I should keep my eyes closed and my mouth open."

"Did you look out for others?"

"Well, I did see a big boat, and something was thrown out right over me, and—"

"I hope you didn't eat any junk food," Father Whale interrupted.

"I'm not sure," Little Whale answered. "I ate one of those funny creatures with no fins or gills. It didn't even taste good."

"What!" cried Father Whale. "Do you realize that you ate a Human?"

"Well, if I did," Little Whale whined, "he's sitting on my liver."

"I am ashamed of you," Father Whale thundered. "You have eaten an endangered species. How could you do such a terrible, disgusting thing?"

Little Whale collapsed on the ocean floor, moaning and groaning.

"What is going on here?" Mother Whale asked.

"Your son," Father Whale bellowed, "has eaten an endangered species and brought shame and sorrow down upon his family."

"Oh, go blow off some steam," said Mother Whale. "Can't you see how sick Little Whale is? Who cares about one nasty, silly Human?" (And she didn't really know just how silly Jonah was.)

She wrapped Little Whale up in seaweed. She fed him a tincture of oyster shells, anemone hearts, and spiny sea urchins. For three days and three nights, Little Whale moaned and groaned as the Human inside him wandered carelessly over his kidneys, spleen, gallbladder, and other tender parts.

Mother Whale changed the medication. She fed Little Whale an embrocation of herring tails, sea serpents, and weakfish oil. And on the fourth morning, Little Whale stopped moaning. He shivered and shook.

"How are you, Little Whale?"
his mother asked anxiously.
Little Whale's eyes bulged.
"Just swim up to the top," his
mother urged, "away from home,
and let it all out, dear. You'll
feel much better."

Little Whale did what his mother told him. He rose up to the top of the waters, and he let it all out. (What happened to Jonah is another story.)

"I feel much better now," he told his mother, "and after this, I'll always keep my eyes open and my mouth closed. I'll look out for others. And I'll never, never eat any more junk food."

"Just listen to your father," said Mother Whale.

"And your mother, too," added Father Whale. "And I hope the Human will do the same."

"People's Gardens": Frederick Law Olmsted and the First Public Parks

·

BY *Milton Meltzer*

·

ILLUSTRATED BY *Kay Chorao*

What would America's cities be like without their public parks?

I try to imagine my town, New York. No Central Park? No Prospect Park? No Riverside Park? Think of your own city with its high buildings, crowded streets, noisy traffic eating up every foot of ground. And not a patch of quiet for relief, not a grove of trees, a stretch of meadow, a bed of flowers, a playground or bicycle path or walkway . . .

Today, however, there's scarcely a city that lacks a public park. But none of them just grew. They had to be created. And one man was responsible for discovering the need, designing the space to fulfill that need, and organizing the huge effort to get the job done.

His name was Frederick Law Olmsted. To him and his partner, Calvert Vaux, America owes many of the parks across the country that have offered us pleasure and beauty for the last one hundred and fifty years.

Where did the idea of a park come from? In the early 1800s New York was already a "tumultuous and brutal city," packed into the lower part of the island of Manhattan. Businessmen were bent on buying up and making a profit from every square foot of the city's tight space. If this kept on, some feared, masses of New Yorkers would be crowded to death. It was a few thoughtful people, led by the poet and newspaper editor William Cullen Bryant and the writer Washington Irving, who imagined what a great open space could do to bring light and air and peace and quiet to the harried souls of the great city. And especially to the children.

For ten years such public-minded citizens campaigned for the city to acquire a large tract as yet untouched by greedy hands. It was hard going. The rich New Yorkers didn't think the city needed a park. (They could go to the mountains or seashore for escape.) And the poor, they said, didn't even know they needed a park. Finally, against great resistance, in 1856 the land was bought by the city for five million dollars.

The area was a series of such rocky ledges that no developer wanted to invest the money to improve even a small part of it. The only people living there were bands of squatters whose shanties clustered under the shelter of the barren rocks. Unfit for farming, the lower parts were swamped in the overflow of pigsties and slaughterhouses; the stench was sickening.

To prepare the ground for construction of the park a superintendent was needed. Olmsted applied for the position. At thirty-five, he had already tried clerking, farming, sailoring, editing, and publishing. But nothing had brought him great success. He knew something about topographical engineering, had studied scientific farming, and had read widely in the theory of landscape design. On visits to Europe and the British Isles he had seen public parks he admired for the way "art had been employed to obtain from nature such beauty." He had to admit there was nothing in democratic America to compare with these "people's gardens."

Olmsted's open opposition to slavery had led the *New York Times* to send him to the South for two years to report on how slavery affected the region's economy and culture. He concluded that the system of slavery perpetuated crude and harsh frontier conditions lacking in the values of community. But the great Eastern cities, too, bursting with immigrants from rural America and immigrants from Europe, were a raw frontier that needed the humanizing influence of parks. Olmsted's work on a book about his recent Southern experience had just been finished when the Central Park job opened up.

Seeking the influence of prominent citizens, Olmsted managed to win the job. His prospects were not promising. The city's politics were corrupt, the economy seemed headed for trouble, he would be poorly paid, and who knew if he could handle such a job? Only himself. He saw this as the chance to turn his pleasure in the care of land into a way of making a living while doing something for the enjoyment of the public.

At the time, Olmsted did not expect to have a hand in the design of the park. He plunged into the daily round of overseeing the seven hundred men hired to build walls, clear brush, and fill in swamps. The site was so rugged, there was scarcely an acre of level ground. His workers— desperate for jobs because the Panic of 1857 had thrown thousands on the street—had been hired by politicians not for their skills but for their votes at the next election. But Olmsted had a gift for matching men to jobs and organizing team effort. He made the work so interesting and important in their eyes that they gave him their best.

With the ground-clearing work under way, the Park Commission announced a contest for the park's design. Olmsted and his friend Calvert Vaux decided to enter the contest. And they won. They were a great team. Vaux, an architectural planner from England, was more highly trained, but Olmsted had the surveyor's skills and an intimate knowledge of every hollow in the rocks, every open space, every rock ledge.

The two young men tramped the park together, seeing and measuring, dreaming and thinking, visualizing how this wasteland could be transformed into lakes, ponds, meadows, woods. The area the partners had to plan for was already determined. It was a rectangle two and a half miles long (between 59th Street on the south end and 110th Street on the north) and half a mile wide (between Central Park West and Fifth Avenue), a total of eight hundred and forty-three acres. Looking at Central Park today, you would think that its designers had found a beautiful landscape and had luckily preserved it for us. But what they really did was to create scenery in so natural a way that most users of the park believe it was always like that.

They not only accomplished this amazing feat but did it in the most practical and economic way. They brought in gravel cheaply by boat from the upper Hudson, let trees of any size remain, took rock for boardbed from the excavations in the park itself. The overflow from the site's old slaughterhouses made the nearby soil organically rich, and they used it to improve the thinner soil, enhancing the beauty of grass and trees.

They could foresee how swiftly the city would surround the park. People would need it for recreation, for exercise, for socializing. But above all, it was to be scenery, whose charm would gradually and silently come over the city dwellers, whose beauty would enter their souls without their knowing exactly how or when, but going away, they would remember it with a tender joy.

Olmsted gave special attention to children's needs. As well as shelters, arbors, benches, and pavilions that everyone could use, he placed rustic rest houses in several locations especially for mothers with young children. Sheep and lambs were pastured nearby for the children's amusement. Besides the lake for skating, he created ponds for children's boats and ponds for wading.

The park area originally contained small reservoirs for water from the Catskill Mountains. The partners converted them into lawns and built a large new reservoir. They designed curving drives in a north and south circular flow, masking them with trees. They added a long, broad tree-lined promenade, or mall, with a fountain and terrace at one end. From the terrace one could view the lake and

the Ramble beyond. One of the ingenious ideas was the design of four transverse roads to carry city traffic rapidly across the park. The partners had them built below park level in open cuts and tunnels so that they would not spoil the scenery.

In the twenty years of his direct connection to Central Park, "Olmsted was probably never happier and never more himself," wrote his biographer. He personally supervised every bit of work on every foot of ground. Without waiting for the park to be completed, the public began to enjoy it. By the winter of 1858–59 skaters were waltzing and racing over the frozen lake. And in the spring thousands were strolling the park's paths, boating on the lake, and riding on horseback or in carriages along the bridle paths and roads. In June the Ramble was opened, and in July the first concert was performed. By this time Olmsted had nearly four thousand men at work. They built many viaduct arches and seven miles of walk, laid ten miles of drainage pipe, and planted over seventeen thousand trees and shrubs. Olmsted later figured that nearly five million cubic yards of earth and stone had been handled in constructing the park, much of it moved from one part of the site to another.

That fall the Park Commission sent Olmsted abroad to study the design of parks in Europe's great cities. Welcomed as a master of landscape planning, he returned home to be hailed as "the only American expert of the first class on parks." He was confident that what he and Vaux had done equaled or surpassed Europe's parks, and he was brimming with ideas of what more might be done.

With Vaux, Olmsted had founded a new American profession. In years to come the partners would plan several more parks in New York and would be commissioned to design parks in Philadelphia, Boston, Washington, D.C., Detroit, Chicago, and California. To Olmsted we also owe measures taken to preserve the natural settings at Niagara Falls, at Yosemite, and in the Adirondacks. He died in 1903, at the age of eighty-one. But his thoughts on the beauty of the wild and the necessity to preserve it still resonate in the actions of today's environmentalists.

Watchers

•

BY *Joanne Ryder*

•

ILLUSTRATED BY *Leo and Diane Dillon*

In the quiet time
when the bright day
softens, lingers,
we come from the hills.
A young one runs
ahead, dancing
on strong pointed toes,
down the golden slopes.
There is grass here
almost belly high
and leafy vines that snake
their way under tall trees.
The young one finds
the shady place first
and dips her long brown head,
snipping and chewing
the sweet green leaves.

In the quiet time
between light and dark,
we stretch our long necks
and watch others passing,
the day ones who come
and go, come and go
along the winding line
where nothing grows.
Our long ears turn,
turn toward them
as they call noisily
to each other.
We sniff.
We smell them.
We watch them
until the tall one stops
along the brown dead line
and calls the others
to turn, to see us
watching them.
Softly, we move away
following no path
but our own.
Secretly, we wait,
we watch these ones
who come and go.

We listen as they kick
the dusty earth
with heavy hooves
and disappear,
behind the hills
hiding the sun.

In the grayness
before dark,
this place is ours,
only faint scents
linger like ghosts
upon the wind.

The Deep Green Gift · BY *Rosemary Wells*

God has given us many great gifts and treasures. One of these is our ancient forests, deep green and cool. We can walk in silence on the forests' paths. We dream and sing about their mysteries.

This man works for a timber company. He is paid for cutting down ancient trees. The timber company says the man needs a job to feed his family. This is true. Everyone needs work.

But there can be other jobs for this man. Some jobs could even help the forests instead of killing them.

And once the ancient forests are cut down, they will never come back. We will have no place to walk in silence, to sing or dream about, because we will have destroyed God's gift to us.

Wetlands

•

BY *Seymour Simon*

Bogs, swamps, marshes, and potholes—freshwater wetlands may not have very inviting names, but they are often beautiful places that are the cradle of life for many kinds of animals. Dragonflies and damselflies, pond snails, small fish, painted and spotted turtles, leopard and pickerel frogs, ducks, muskrats, and beavers—all live in wetlands. Mice and snakes often live around the edges of wetlands. Wetlands are also home to one-third of the threatened and endangered species of North American wildlife.

Wetlands are spots where water is at or near the surface of the land. In swamps and marshes, the water level often rises and falls depending upon the season and the amount of rainfall. In bogs, the water may disappear during dry seasons, but the ground usually remains spongy and wet to the touch.

Many wetlands have stretches of open water surrounded by cattails, rushes, and arrowheads, or other plants that grow with their stems and leaves partly underwater. Some plants, such as water lilies, are rooted in the bottom and have their leaves floating on the surface. Duckweed and other floaters spread out on the surface and trail their roots downward into the water. Trees and shrubs, such as red maple, bald cypress, swamp azalea, and spicebush, are able to grow with their roots submerged for long periods of time. Skunk cabbage, marsh marigold, and jewelweed may grow beneath the trees and shrubs.

Wetlands range in size from those that cover only a fraction of an acre to the huge swamps and marshes of Florida, the Carolinas, Georgia, and Louisiana. The large prairie potholes of the midwestern United States and Canada provide nesting places for two-thirds of the more than ten million North American ducks and other waterfowl,

while millions more nest in the swamps and marshes of the southeastern United States.

Wetlands are important to people as well. They act like natural sponges, helping protect against floods. They recycle decaying plant and animal materials and allow the chemicals in them to be used again by living things. Wetlands filter pollutants and cleanse fresh waters better than any sewage-treatment plant ever built. Wetlands are places for fishing and small boats and are also spots of peace and quiet beauty.

But many people still think of wetlands as wastelands and breeding grounds for mosquitoes, flies, and disease. People dump garbage in wetlands, fill them in to use for farming, and pave them over to build shopping centers, airports, and houses. More than half of the two hundred million acres of wetlands that existed during colonial days in what are now the lower forty-eight states have since vanished. Scientists estimate that more than one thousand acres of wetlands are lost every day, half a million acres a year.

Many people and nature organizations are working to save our remaining wetlands. All of us can help, too, by learning about our local wetlands and telling our friends and families about how wonderful wetlands really are and how they need to be protected. You may not want to live in a swamp or a bog, but wetlands are some of the world's most interesting places to explore and treasure.

Pigs on Patrol · BY *David McPhail*

Pigs on patrol protect the planet.
If something's harmful, pigs will ban it.
On land and sea and in the air,
Patrolling pigs are everywhere.

Patrolling piggies pick up trash—
Cans and bottles bring in cash.
Garbage makes a tasty treat—
It gives the pigs a lot to eat.

Patrolling piggies don't like litter.
It makes them mad, it makes them bitter.
When they see a paper cup,
They bend right down and pick it up.

Pigs patrolling in the woods
Will try and catch you with the goods.
Pick a flower you shouldn't touch,
And they won't like it very much.

Patrolling piggies save the whales
By tying ropes around their tails
And pulling till the whales are free.
Then they tow them out to sea.

The sight of seabirds doused with oil
Causes piggies' blood to boil.
They wash the birds and pat them dry,
Then return them to the sky.

A smokestack spews some smelly gases
As a pig patrolling passes.
Up the stack the piggy goes,
Holding tight his piggy nose.
At the top he whirls around,
Gives a grunt and then sits down,
Plugging up the sooty stack,
Sending all the gases back.

On all tankers, and barges too,
Pigs patrol disguised as crew.
When they spot a spreading slick,
They beat the captain with a stick.

Pigs patrolling land and sea
Need some help from you and me.
Let's join the piggies on patrol—
Come save the Earth and keep it whole.

The Earth Game

·

BY *Pam Conrad*

·

ILLUSTRATED BY *Diane Goode*

Not very long ago, in a meadow not too far from here, some children found a ball of twine lying in the grass.

"Watch me," called the oldest girl. And she tied the end of the string to her finger and tossed the ball in the air.

Her brother caught it and wrapped the string around his own finger. Then he pitched it across to his friend.

The twine unwound just enough as it sailed through the air. His friend caught the ball, wrapped the string around his thumb, and threw it over to someone else.

After many tosses back and forth, the ball had unwound to just a loose end, and the smallest child wound that around his finger. And there they were, joined in a circle by the twine that wove a net at their center.

"Now look," said the oldest girl, and she wiggled her finger.

"I felt that!" said her brother.

"So did I," said his friend.

And standing very still, one by one, they each wiggled a finger until they could feel the twine move with even the gentlest tug.

"Now, let's be the Earth," said the girl. She closed her eyes, and her voice lifted over the meadow. "I am a jungle in Africa, and someone is shooting an elephant for his tusks." She moved her finger. They all felt the tug and grew sad.

"I'm the Arctic Ocean," said her brother, "and an oil tanker is hitting an iceberg and spilling oil over me. Soon all the birds will be black and slick and won't fly anymore." He tugged, and they were silent.

"I am a big city, and no one can see the stars in the sky because the air is thick with smoke and fumes from my factories." The gentle tug passed around them.

"I was once a farm, but the sunflowers and rows of corn are gone. Today I am a mall." They each felt the sad tug.

They stopped tugging. It was as though a thick cloud had passed before the sun and darkened their day. It was very still, except for a bird whizzing by over their heads.

Then the smallest boy smiled. He moved his finger. "I'm a town, and in a backyard somebody's putting out seed for the winter birds." He tugged again, and their faces lit up.

"Yes!" The tallest girl raised her hands, and the pull was felt by all. "I'm a highway, and people are walking alongside me, picking up bottles and cans for recycling." She wiggled her fingers and laughed, and they could all feel it.

"I'm a neighborhood, and people are planting trees along my concrete sidewalks."

"I am an ocean, and fishermen are freeing the dolphins from their nets."

"I'm a herd of wild mustangs, and someone has given me land and turned me loose."

"I'm a lonely country road, and somebody's painting my mailbox red."

They all laughed. Then they raised their hands, lifting the net of twine higher and higher. They could feel the certain pull of all the things people could do to make a better world.

And that is how—not too long ago, in a meadow not very far from here—a ball of twine was the beginning of the Earth game.

When we were around, we didn't burn, destroy, litter, or pollute. And we left the world the way we found it! LOOK WHAT YOU'VE GONE AND DONE! Now run and tell your friends to STOP. SAVE THIS GREAT PLANET!
WE WILL!
HURRY!

Three Cheers for Bats!

·

BY *Laurence Pringle*

·

PHOTOGRAPHS BY *Merlin D. Tuttle*

To many people, bats are scary, ugly creatures. The superstitions about them range from tales of Dracula-type vampires to the belief that they entangle themselves in people's hair. These notions about bats are still common; no wonder bats are still feared and persecuted in many lands.

These old beliefs are disappearing, however, as people learn about the lives of *real* bats. About a thousand kinds of bats live on all continents except Antarctica. None are blind, and some see very well. Large fruit-eating bats that live in the tropics have big eyes and doglike snouts. They're called flying foxes.

Most bats are insect eaters, and they are the ones with weird faces. They usually have big ears and sometimes have odd-looking noses. With their beady little eyes they see as well as mice or other small mammals. To catch food in the dark, though, they rely on a sonar, or echo-location, system that is more advanced than anything devised by people. In fact, scientists still don't understand many details of this extraordinary system.

The bats emit high-pitched squeaks that we cannot hear. Some of these sounds echo off objects in front of the flying bats: tree branches, wires, flying insects. Bats listen to the echoes and get an instantaneous and changing picture in their brains of what lies ahead. They dodge twigs and other obstacles. They zoom in on moths and even tiny mosquitoes.

The odd-looking noses and ears of some bats are part of their sonar equipment. Their echolocation system works beautifully. Bats can and do easily avoid getting tangled in a person's hair. When they sometimes swoop near people who are outdoors at night, they are often chasing mosquitoes, which they pluck out of the air before the insects can feast on the humans.

*Pallid bat in flight
with a katydid*

*California leaf-nosed bat
flying to a cricket*

Roosting Indian
flying fox

Where mosquitoes are abundant, a small bat can catch several hundred in an hour. People who know this take steps to encourage bats to live near their home. They put up specially designed bat houses in which bats can rest in the daytime.

Bats can eat an astonishing number of flying insects. In Austin, Texas, a colony of nearly a million free-tailed bats consumes from fifteen to thirty thousand pounds of insects each summer night. People in the Austin area are proud of their bats and celebrate their return each summer.

Farther west, long-nosed bats feed on nectar within cactus flowers. The cacti, including the giant saguaro, bloom only at night. As the bats fly from one flower to another, dipping their noses deep inside, they also carry pollen from flower to flower. Without long-nosed bats, saguaros and other large cacti could not produce seeds.

In East Africa, the giant baobab tree also is pollinated by bats. Its large white flowers open at night, an invitation to nectar-feeding bats. The baobab is called the "tree of life" because so many other plants and animals depend on it for their survival. Without bats, however, baobabs themselves would eventually die out. For the baobab, bats are the "mammals of life."

In tropical rain forests, flying foxes and other bats also are important pollinators. Fruit-eating bats play another vital role: Seeds from the fruit pass quickly through their digestive tracts and are expelled in flight. In this way, tree seeds are scattered in rain forests. When fruit bats fly over cleared land where agriculture has been abandoned, the seeds they drop make forest regrowth possible.

As the vital roles of bats in nature become better known, more and more people work to protect these creatures. Bats often rest or raise their young in caves or other shelters where they can easily be found and destroyed. In the United States, some bat colonies are now protected from disturbance. Metal gates have been built across the openings to their cave homes. People are kept out, and the bats can fly freely in and out.

Bats are intelligent and gentle. Their fur feels wonderfully soft to the touch. When people see a bat, they are often tempted to pick it up. This is not wise. Bats naturally hide in the daytime, and any bat that is not hidden may be sick. It may be dying of a disease called rabies that can be transmitted to humans through a bite. Never touch a bat that seems sick or injured.

If we leave bats alone, and leave their caves and other homes alone, they will thrive and continue to be some of the most fascinating and beneficial mammals on Earth. Hurrah for bats!

Why There Is Death

A NATIVE AMERICAN STORY

•

ADAPTED BY *John Bierhorst*

•

ILLUSTRATED BY *Wendy Watson*

In the beginning of the world there was no such thing as death. Everyone kept on living. Finally there were so many people, there was no more room on the Earth.

The people's leaders held a meeting to decide what to do. One man stood up and said it would be a good plan to have people die, but just for a while, and then they would come back to life.

As soon as the man sat down, Coyote jumped up and said, "No, that's not right. People should die forever. This little world is not large enough to hold everyone. If the people who died came back to life, there would not be enough food for them to eat."

The others objected. "We do not want our friends and relatives to die and be gone forever. There would be too much sadness." All except Coyote agreed that death would last for only a while.

Then the doctors built a large medicine lodge facing east. When they had finished it, they called everyone together and announced that they would invite the ghosts of the dead and make them live again. The people were glad.

When all was ready, the first person died. Then the doctors sat down in the medicine lodge and began to sing, inviting the dead person's ghost. In about ten days a whirlwind blew in from the west and circled the lodge.

Coyote was watching. He knew the ghost was inside the whirlwind. When the whirlwind was about to go into the lodge, Coyote ran and closed the door. Seeing that the door was closed, the ghost whirled on by. And in that moment, death began forever.

From then on, when the people saw a whirlwind or heard the wind whistle, they would say, "Someone is wandering." Because ever since Coyote closed the door, the

ghosts of the dead have wandered across the Earth. They go this way and that way, until at last they find the road to the Spirit Land.

And Coyote? The people are still angry at him. That's why he keeps running away, looking back first over one shoulder and then over the other, to see if anyone is chasing him. He is always lean and hungry and has to catch what he can, because no one will help him or give him anything to eat.

Note: In many Native American tribes two kinds of stories are told. One kind is for entertainment only. The other, more serious kind is said to have taken place "long ago" or "in the beginning." These more serious stories tell how the Earth got to be the way it is today and why people must sometimes accept hard choices if human life is to continue. The tale about Coyote and why there is death is an "in the beginning" story from the Caddo, a Great Plains tribe related to the Pawnee and the Wichita. Formerly of Louisiana and Texas, the Caddo today live in western Oklahoma. Sources for the story: George A. Dorsey, *Traditions of the Caddo*, Carnegie Institution of Washington, 1905; Margot Astrov, *The Winged Serpent*, John Day, 1946.

Bird

·

BY *Stephanie S. Tolan*

·

ILLUSTRATED BY *Ted Rand*

"Might as well put the cage away," Mom said when I got home from school that warm September day. "She's gone for good."

The chicken-wire-and-wood cage sat on the picnic table on our back deck, looking so empty it was hard to believe she'd ever been inside, whistling and chucking at me, making demands. I'd filled the cup with fresh food that morning, same as I had every day for the week she'd been gone. Just in case. But Mom was probably right. Bird didn't need me anymore.

I sat down on the picnic bench, remembering the day I'd found her, a little round ball of sooty gray down, under the red-tipped bush by the back door. Mr. Malcolm's big ginger tom was watching her through the fence between our yards. I couldn't find the nest to put her back and didn't dare leave her for her parents to feed on the ground. That tom would have been over the fence in a flash. Or Circe, our long-haired black cat, would have found her.

I told Mom and Dad she was a mockingbird. How was I to know? The closest thing she had to feathers were those little gray quills sticking out, making her look something like a scruffed-up hedgehog. Anyway, it didn't matter. I fed her what my book said to feed any baby bird—strained meats and dry cat food soaked in milk-and-egg formula. That first day she opened her yellow-edged beak like the Grand Canyon and yelled when anything near her moved. In no time, though, she figured out who I was and only called for food when I came close.

So I knew she was supersmart. Later, when her feathers came in, she was fast at learning to fly, too. A couple of times she fluttered off my hand and made a crash landing on the floor. Then she got good enough to fly from one hand to the other. Before the end of that day she could fly clear up to the curtain rod over my window and back down to my hand again.

First time I took her out in the yard, she set right out to find bugs, running around in the grass, spreading the blades with her beak. Only she didn't know what to do next. So I brought some big black ants into my room and let them go on the rug. She'd chase them down and open her mouth right over them, but she didn't know enough to close it again. Scared me. I sure couldn't teach her how.

But she figured it out on her own—just snapped one up one day and gobbled it down. She had learned to bite. Practiced on my fingers and ears after that. She used to try to pull the tufts off my bedspread. And she was always checking under my collar or in the wadded-up socks on my floor—in case bugs might live in there.

By this time she was getting pretty big—dark gray but stubby tailed, with no white on her wings. *Not* a mockingbird. I found her in the bird book. Adults are purplish green, spotted in the winter. But young ones are gray till mating time. I gritted my teeth when I told Mom and Dad, "Starling."

"Oh, no!" Dad said. "Starlings are worthless! We're not saving any junk bird." He threw up his hands. "Half the country is trying to get rid of starlings, and my son's raising one."

That's when I looked up her scientific name. I thought

it would be so elegant she'd feel proud, plus it might help me argue with Dad. So much for that great idea. *Sturnus vulgaris.* The first part just means starling; the other means common.

"She's common, all right," Dad said. "There must be trillions of starlings, gobbling up crops and fruit, stealing from other birds, gumming up airplane engines. Nuisance birds! Pests! Worse than pigeons!"

Mom didn't help much. She told me about towns that spend lots of time and money trying to get rid of their starlings. They make noises to scare them away, or poison them or shoot them. Sometimes they spray them with detergent so they'll lose the insulation in their feathers and freeze to death at night.

It made me sick. So I went to the library and read up on starlings.

Pretty depressing. Most of what I found was on Dad's side. There aren't many birds people hate more. Even bird people hate them. It isn't that starlings are bad, just that there are so many of them. The thing is, they're only here in America because some guy brought some over from England and turned them loose in Central Park, New York City, in 1890. He released a bunch of other English birds, too, all because he had this idea that it would be neat to have every bird Shakespeare ever mentioned living in America. The trouble with that idea was that English birds couldn't make it over here. They all died out, except the starlings. In less than fifty years starlings had spread all the way across the country and into Canada, too.

Then I got mad. What happened wasn't the starlings' fault. They didn't ask to get brought to America. All they did was survive—mostly because they were smart. Starlings have really big brains, so big they can learn to talk —like parrots—and they can imitate any other bird's song. Noises, too, like squeaky doors and police whistles.

When people dumped them on a new continent, they had to learn to migrate to new places. They were mostly country birds, but they figured out that cities are warm in the winter, so lots of them started staying in town, flying out in the morning to find food in the fields, then back in the evening to roost on warm buildings. Mom calls them "bird blobs" when they fly all together like that. Seems to me it's pretty impressive that they don't crash into each other.

They had to learn to eat different food in America, too. Scientists figure they watched other birds to see what was good to eat. Now they eat just about everything: bugs, seeds, acorns, snails, even leaves and garbage if they have to. When I found out starlings eat millions of Japanese beetles every year, I figured that would win Dad over. He thinks *they're* a nuisance, too.

But he was not impressed. He still wanted me to get

rid of her. "Pests," he kept saying. "Worthless."

"Smart," I said. "And tough."

Then one day Circe was lying on the family-room floor in the sun, one paw over her nose. She was purring in her sleep, the tip of her tail twitching. Bird was on the floor, too, picking bits of lint off the rug. She cocked her head and looked at Circe. Then she stomped—really, *stomped*—across the floor and bit Circe's tail. That cat rose straight up in the air with a yowl and hit the ground running. She was out of the room in a streak of black. Bird looked up at Dad, who was sitting on the couch, and sort of fluffed her feathers. Then she settled herself in the spot of sun, just where Circe had been, and closed her eyes.

"Tough," Dad admitted.

She lived on the deck for a few weeks in the cage Dad and I built. I'd leave the door open so she could come and go. She'd hang around the yard, or even disappear during the day, then come back and let me close the cage at night. I kept a cup of mynah-bird food there for her, which she liked maybe better than bugs.

One night she didn't come back. It's what was supposed to happen; you can't just keep wild birds. But that didn't make it easy. I missed her coming down to my shoulder, sticking her beak in my ear, whistling and fussing at me. And I didn't know if she was okay. What if she'd gone after some strange cat? Worse, what if there were people out there shooting and poisoning "pests"?

Now, sitting there thinking about that, I didn't feel like putting her cage away. So I went inside to get a snack.

I was coming back through the sliding glass doors with a peanut butter and banana sandwich when I heard her voice. Unmistakable. And there she was on the bottom branch of the maple tree. I stayed where I was, hardly daring to breathe. Next to her was a stranger, a shiny black male starling.

She chucked a couple of times and flew down to her cage. Then she hopped inside and gobbled a piece of mynah-bird food. She chucked louder. The male dropped down and landed on the open door of the cage. But he wouldn't go in. She whistled and chucked. Finally, looking as if he'd rather be anyplace else in the world, that male hopped inside. He looked around, cocking his head one way, then another, and took off again, straight up to the maple branch. She took another bite of food and flew up to join him. Right away, he took off.

She stayed on that branch for a second, looking down at the cage, and then she flew after him. I guess he'd seen what she wanted him to see. I had to laugh. Even if I never saw Bird again, I figured now it was okay.

I'm no bird expert, but one thing I know. *Sturnus vulgaris* may be common, *Sturnus vulgaris* may even be a pest. But worthless? No way!

Note: Though this is a fictionalized version, Bird was a very real starling who lived with the author and her family and did all these things!

Prayer for Earth

•

BY *Myra Cohn Livingston*

•

ILLUSTRATED BY *Debra Frasier*

Last night
an owl
called from the hill.
Coyotes howled.
A deer stood still,
nibbling at bushes far away.
The moon shone silver.
Let this stay.

Today
two noisy crows
flew by,
their shadows pasted to the sky.
The sun broke out
through clouds of grey.
An iris opened.
Let this stay.

Limericks

·

BY *X. J. Kennedy*

·

ILLUSTRATED BY *Quentin Blake*

Said an earthworm to me, "Beg your pardon,
May I bore a few holes in your garden?
　　It may seem to you odd
　　That I'd chew through a clod,
But I don't want our planet to harden."

Said the mom of the baby blue shark,
"Try that beach at the national park.
    You'll have wonderful fun
    Making everyone run—
Just be sure, dear, you're home before dark."

Letter from Crinkleroot

·

BY *Jim Arnosky*

Hello!

My name is Crinkleroot. I was born in a tree and raised by bees! My home is the forest, but I've been to the desert and walked in the sea. I've climbed hills and mountains and explored river valleys. Wherever I go, I go on foot, so I can always feel the Earth under me.

On my walks, I look for all the other creatures that share the Earth. Already I've seen more animals than I can count. Well, yes, I can count them. I've seen one billion six million two thousand four hundred and three and two-thirds (if you count the lizard that lost its tail!). And I'm still counting.

To do the job right, to see all the living things for whom the Earth is home, I'd have to search in every backyard and woodlot, look up every tree, and peek down every hole. I'd have to examine up close every crack in every rock and pavement. I'd need to look everywhere on land and underwater.

I'm not sure I'll be able to get to all these places and see every living thing. But I'm going to try. And every time I find something—a bird or

bug or wildflower or fern—I haven't seen before, I'll tell everyone I meet. Then they will know how rich and wonderful the planet Earth is!

It's such a big job, I'll need some help. Perhaps you can talk to your friends and your family about any creatures you see in your own neighborhood. We can all find and see a great many things. We can learn and share a lot.

So keep your eyes open and your nose poked out. Maybe we'll bump into one another somewhere in the great outdoors.

Your friend,

Crinkleroot

Traffic

•

BY *William Sleator*

At 5:30 A.M. Sandy spotted the big pink Mercedes at
the corner of Avenue 253. Wearing gloves in the blazing
heat, he maneuvered his metal food cart, which would
have been too hot to touch with bare hands, around the
motionless belching cars and trucks, always on the alert
for motorcycle gas vendors weaving between the trapped
lanes. All the cars had their own little refrigerators and

microwaves, but there were some car people who were cautious about using up their food supplies, not knowing how long they would have to make them last. These were Sandy's customers.

He was in luck. The swarms of vendors hadn't reached the Mercedes yet. And the car was directly behind an eighteen-wheeler, its windshield already coated by the truck's dense black emissions. Sandy waved his windshield cleaner at the woman inside the Mercedes, who was on the phone. Car people were always on the phone. That was how they communicated with one another, since there was rarely more than one person in a car.

When she noticed him, he lifted five fingers and pointed at her windshield. Her expression was hesitant; she was not experienced in traffic. He tried his most winning smile and bowed. She smiled and nodded shyly at him.

He knew the car wouldn't be moving for a while, but he did the windshield quickly, eager to get to other cars. She opened the window only a couple of inches to slip him the five. But that was enough for him to feel a shivery caress of cool, fragrant air from inside. "Coffee, madam?" he said politely, changing his gloves. "Only seven bucks." He gestured to show that his cart, though old and dented, was clean, the food protected by the plastic cover. The gesture also implied that he had no weapon; car people were scared of the streets.

She rolled down the window a little more. Oh, was it comfortable inside the cars, the coolness and the spacious empty seats! The woman, clean and pretty, was even wearing a sweater! She smiled again when he presented the coffee to her with a flourish—he had learned that being a ham helped him with customers. She seemed pleased—and surprised—when he instantly gave her three bucks change. Only 5:45, and he'd made twelve bucks already!

By noon the Mercedes had progressed two blocks, down to Avenue 251. "She's moving right along," said his friend Rusty, a water vendor. "Let's hit her for lunch," he whispered, so the other vendors packed tightly around them wouldn't hear.

The Mercedes lady seemed happy to see him again, her smile friendlier. He made sure she saw that he was wearing two pairs of plastic gloves, the inner pair clean enough to handle the plastic-wrapped sandwiches and pastries. (The gloves also hid the open sores on his hands.) Fifteen bucks for a ham-and-cheese on rye and a Danish; and Rusty sold her a bottle of water for eight.

They were doing so well that they took a break, squatting for a smoke in the dense coughing crowd in front of the abandoned building where they lived. They were all kids here—no one who worked on the streets ever got very old. The sun was fierce; their drenched sooty T-shirts clung to their skin. Hundreds of street vendors slept in this building, but no one could figure out why it had ever been constructed: There were only stairways and broken-down elevators inside, and no ramps at all! Why would anybody make a building without ramps?

By 5:00 P.M. the Mercedes was down to the light at Avenue 245. The car lady was probably hungry again. He had to wait while she dealt with a gas vendor. Though the cars rarely moved, the car people could never turn off their engines. If they did, they would have no air-conditioning, no refrigerators or TVs. Fuel was expensive, and the gas vendors, sleek and powerful, did very good business.

She only bought a little gas, and soon the motorcycle buzzed away, spitting exhaust into the haze. With elaborate, humorous gestures, Sandy showed the car lady his food again. She smiled briefly at his performance, then shook her head, looking worried. And she didn't even open the window—Sandy would have loved another gust of that cold air! But the car lady gestured that she was out of cash. And the vendors, operating on the fringes of legality, couldn't take credit cards. She was in trouble, all right; she had used her last money to buy a small amount of fuel. Sandy moved away.

The Mercedes was no longer a customer, but Sandy

still kept his eye on her as he wearily pushed and turned his heavy cart back and forth in the sweltering fumes. Food carts were narrow so that, like motorcycles, they could fit between the lanes, but their shape made them awkward to handle. At 8:00 P.M. the Mercedes was still at Avenue 245. There was a problem somewhere. Nothing was moving at all.

At 8:30 the Mercedes began honking. Sandy thought fast. She wasn't going to buy anything; whatever was happening with the Mercedes, his cart would only be in the way. He got it back to the building and locked it up, then hurried around the traffic for the Mercedes, spitting frequently, wiping his forehead with toilet paper to try to get rid of some of the grime. The car's headlights were off! Sandy wedged his way through the vendors crowding around the honking Mercedes and pressed his face against the window.

The car lady nodded at him in relief and beckoned. The back-door lock clicked open. Hard as it was to believe, she was inviting him inside! Maybe she trusted him because he had quickly given her change—and because of his amusing manner. The others would have fought him for the chance to get in, but they couldn't desert their carts. Sandy pulled open the door and slammed it behind him.

It was hotter inside the car than outside. "Please, can

you help me?" the woman said, fanning her face with one hand, her frantic eyes meeting his in the rearview mirror. She seemed sick now, breathing shallowly in the ovenlike heat. "I didn't believe it was really this bad downtown. I've got to get to my husband in the hospital. But I'm out of gas, out of cash, and my phone's dead. I don't know what to do."

"First open the windows or we'll fry. Just a couple of inches. They won't be able to get in."

"But the pollution! People can't . . ." She faltered, as though realizing for the first time that Sandy *did* breathe on the city streets. Luckily the windows could be operated manually. They rolled them down a few inches, letting in what passed for a breeze and the rich, oily traffic smell, the smell Sandy lived with and barely noticed—except for the whiff of its absence from car windows.

"I guess it's a little cooler," the lady said, her hand over her nose and mouth. "Can you think of any way to help me?" She looked worse now, her face strangely pale. She sank back against the seat. "Please, try to—" She choked, tears running down her cheeks. She slumped forward.

Nothing like this had ever happened to Sandy before. It was like a dream! The car lady was out cold; Sandy guessed the air must be different out where she lived. It took him a while to roll her limp body into the passenger's seat. Maybe she'd wake up later, maybe she wouldn't. But the keys were in the ignition.

Sandy slid into the driver's seat, his heart thudding with excitement. He had forty bucks in his pocket, earnings from yesterday and today. He stuck his arm out the window and signaled for gas.

Forty dollars' worth of gas wasn't a lot, but he didn't care. For however long it held out, *he* would be a car person, watching TV in icy isolated luxury. He could brag about it for the rest of his life.

We Are Plooters

·

BY *Jack Prelutsky*

·

ILLUSTRATED BY *Paul O. Zelinsky*

We are Plooters,
We don't care,
We make messes
Everywhere,
We strip forests
Bare of trees,
We dump garbage
In the seas.
　　　We are Plooters,
　　　We enjoy
　　　Finding beauty
　　　To destroy,
　　　We intrude
　　　Where creatures thrive,
　　　Soon there's little
　　　Left alive.
　　　　　Underwater,
　　　　　Underground,
　　　　　Nothing's safe
　　　　　When we're around,
　　　　　We spew poisons
　　　　　In the air,
　　　　　We are Plooters,
　　　　　We don't care.

From Island to Island

·

B Y *Lynne Cherry*

This is the story my grandmother told me once long ago when I was a child. We were on a boat sailing across the sea, looking for a new home.

When I was a little girl like you, she began, I lived on Great Coral Island. Once our home had been a place of beauty. But all the islanders had many children, and little by little the people cut down the forests. Then the sun scorched the earth, the water dried up, and the crops withered and died.

So our family sailed off, looking for a new place to live. We sailed for many days, and I was afraid that we would never find land. But at last an island appeared on the horizon. It sat like a jewel in the vast green sea, shimmering a deep, dark emerald green.

We landed on the island and found clear streams that provided water and rivers teeming with fish.

We named it Emerald Island.

Our families grew as the years went by, until a hundred people lived on Emerald Island. Each person drank the island's water, ate the island's fruit, and cut down the island's trees for houses and firewood.

I grew up and married and myself had ten children. By then most of the trees were gone, and the island was baked by the sun. Emerald Island was no longer green. The crops withered and turned brown. There was no longer enough for everybody. I did not have food to feed my children. I lost five of them and my husband to hunger.

Emerald Island had become too crowded. By the time you were born, there were hundreds of people living there—on a barren island. There has never been enough for you to eat. You children know hunger all too well. And that is why thirty of us have decided to leave Emerald Island and look for a new place to live.

That was the end of my grandmother's story.

We had lost sight of Emerald Island within a few hours. For days we sailed. Like my grandmother so many years before, I was afraid that we would not find another island. Nobody knew where we were going. We just followed the winds. Finally we saw land.

We arrived at a large island and stared in wonder at the beauty of the green forest. Fish filled the streams of cool water that rushed through the forest. The trees were heavy with fruit. We called it Hope Island.

The next few years on Hope Island were indeed full of hope and happiness. For the first time in my life I always had enough to eat!

I grew up and married a fine young man. We had a daughter. Other people had children, too. There were now eighty people on the island. Many of the trees had been cut, so there was not much fruit. The streams did not rush through the forest as fast, and they were not full of fish. Still, we were full of hope.

But one evening, my grandmother asked everyone to gather together. She told us that she probably did not have much time left to live and there was something she wanted to say before she died.

My daughter sat at her feet as I had done so many years before, when I was a little girl. My grandmother told of how, as a child, she and her parents had sailed away from the parched Great Coral Island. She told of finding Emerald Island, so lush and green, with food and water for all, and of her sadness upon leaving it, crowded, brown, parched, and dry.

"We ruined Emerald Island," she said. "We made it a desert, and now we are doing the same to Hope Island. *There are too many of us.* Fewer people would use less wood and less water. Fewer people would eat less fruit and fish. There would be enough for all—for us, our children, and our children's children."

When my grandmother finished, there was silence. Then my daughter spoke: "Mother and Father, we're so happy—just the three of us. Could our family stay the same?"

I looked at her and at my grandmother. "Yes," I answered. "Our family is just the right size for a family on Hope Island."

That night my grandmother died, but her words stayed with us. We have been on Hope Island for fifty years. Now I am the wise old woman of the island. Each year I tell my grandmother's story of sailing from island to island. We seventy Hope Islanders are happy and well fed. Our island shimmers a deep, dark green, like a jewel in the vast green sea. There is a bright future for our children and our children's children on Hope Island.

The Boy Who Loved to Swim

·

BY *Jean Craighead George*

·

ILLUSTRATED BY *Barbara Cooney*

A boy who loved to swim once lived in a small house by a lively mountain stream.

He could fish and watch birds, but he could not swim. The stream was too shallow. It cascaded over rocks and skimmed above logs.

One day he took matters into his own hands and built a dam.

As the water rose, it covered the roots of the ancient birch trees that grew along the stream. They suffocated and died. It flooded the forest floor, and the wildflowers drowned. With no trees or ground plants the birds could not nest. They flew away.

But the pool behind the dam was deep and clear, and the boy swam for hours and hours. He dived and rolled onto his back and enjoyed the open sky.

The sun poured down and warmed the water. The trout, who needed cold water, died. With no trout to eat them, the water insects multiplied. Now when the boy went swimming, he was brutally bitten by mosquitoes.

Up the mountain, the swift stream still behaved as always. It eroded the rocks and made silt. The silt would have been carried downhill to the river delta, but now the dam stopped it. The silt began filling the pool. Before long the boy couldn't dive without hitting the bottom.

Like all dams, this dam began to leak. The boy built it higher. The water flooded more forest and more trees died.

One day the miller, who lived downstream, paid a visit to the boy.

"Your dam has cut off the water to my mill," he said. "With no water to turn the wheel, I cannot make flour. I will soon starve. Please take down your dam."

"This is my land," said the boy. "I can do what I want with it. I want a dam and a pool.

"Besides," he went on. "If I take down the dam, the water behind it will flood the town in the valley."

The miller thought about the people in the valley and agreed that the water would flood their homes.

"Maybe," he said, "we can both be happy. We'll dig a mill race. It will have a floodgate. When you open the gate, the water will flow down to my mill. When you close it, you can swim."

The boy really did not want the miller to starve, so together they dug a mill race.

When the boy opened the gate, the water ran down the race and turned the miller's waterwheel. When he closed it, he swam. But by now the pool had so filled with silt that he could only paddle in it.

One day a group of people from the town came to call on the boy.

"Your dam and the mill race," said their leader, "are causing great hardship. Boats can no longer use the river. Our port and our trade are gone."

The boy did not want to cause hardship. And his pool was so filled with silt that it was too shallow to use even for paddling.

"Very well," he said. "I'll take down my dam."

But when he removed the dam and opened the flood-gate, the water that was left took another course down the mountain. The town still had no port. The miller had no water to turn his wheel.

The boy looked in despair at the muddy gash in the mountain where his pool had been.

And there in the mud he saw a small sprout of green. An acorn was growing in the silt. Near it the mountain stream cascaded along as it used to do.

Trees will grow here again and birds will nest in them, he thought. The trees will cool the water and the trout will return. And if I let things alone, the water will find its old bed and flow past the mill to the town.

"As for me," he said, getting to his feet, "I love to wade."

He stepped into the water and went splashing and singing back to his house.

Me and My Weeds

•

BY *Anne Rockwell*

In the vacant lot next door
all sorts of flowers grow.
Red clover, white Queen Anne's lace,
and purple thistles look up at the sky.
Fuzzy-leaved mulleins and marshmallows
are taller than I am.
Butterflies like the milkweed best.
They come to sip honey from
the clusters of small pink blossoms.
I like cockleburs because
I can make them stick together.
Sometimes they stick to me.
And I know a secret about buttercups.
If you hold one under someone's chin
and the petals stay shiny,
that person loves someone
but won't tell who.
But best of all,
I like dandelions.

Their yellow flowers turn into
white, fluffy balls.
Then I can blow the seeds away.
My father says all those flowers
in the vacant lot next door
are really weeds,
because nobody planted them there.
But I call them flowers
just the same.

Elliot's House

•

BY *Lois Lowry*

All of the children in Ms. McKreutzer's classroom drew pictures of their own homes. There were condos, apartments, farmhouses, ranch houses, and split-levels, and one little girl—her name was Alvinia—drew a mansion with seven chimneys and a gazebo.

"We certainly do live in all sorts of places, don't we, class?" Ms. McKreutzer said. She hung the pictures on the wall.

From time to time the children made changes on their pictures. "We got new curtains," Elizabeth said, and she added yellow curtains to the windows of her house.

"New car," Alvinia said. She added a stretch limo to the front of her mansion.

A boy named Elliot had drawn a picture of an ordinary house. Elliot's house had a chimney, a door, four windows, a fence, a front walk, and a tree. Now, beside the door, he added a lumpy mound of something brownish green.

"What's that?" the children asked.

"Garbage," Elliot told them.

"Is it waiting there to be collected?" Ms. McKreutzer asked.

"No," Elliot said. "It's where we keep it. We throw it out this window." He pointed to the window beside the door of the house. "We like to do it that way," he explained.

"My goodness," said Ms. McKreutzer.

A boy named David recolored his house one day. It had been white. Now it was red. "We painted our house," he explained.

Elizabeth added some flowering plants to her yard. "Zinnias," she said.

Alvinia added bushes around her swimming pool. "New landscaping," she announced.

Elliot added several more mounds. They covered the

first window, and he added others below another window. "More garbage," he announced, even though no one had asked. He drew black dots above the mounds.

"Flies," he explained.

"My goodness," Ms. McKreutzer said.

Each day Elliot added something new to his picture. He added a large white rectangle. "Old broken-down refrigerator," he explained.

He added some silvery ovals near the front walk. "Dead fish," he said. Then he added cats.

Tires.

Cars without tires.

Mice. Or maybe they were rats.

And the garbage mounds grew higher.

"All of your windows are covered up now," Ms. McKreutzer said one day. "How do you get sunlight?"

"It's dark inside," Elliot said. "We like it that way."

"How do you get into your house?" the other children asked. "The front walk is covered with dead fish and broken appliances."

"We climb," Elliot explained. "And dig tunnels. We like it that way."

David added a baby carriage to his picture after his mom had a new baby. To hers, Alvinia added three gray curly-haired dogs, walking in a row. "Champion poodles," she said.

The rest of the class smiled politely and said, "Nice." But they weren't really interested in David's new baby brother or Alvinia's dogs. They were all very interested in Elliot's house. They watched his picture each day to see what Elliot would add next.

Carefully Elliot drew a round orange thing in the branches of his tree.

"Frisbee?" Ms. McKreutzer asked.

Elliot shook his head. "Pizza," he said. "It was on the kitchen table for a week and started getting moldy. So we threw it out of an upstairs window."

He took a pencil and made black dots all over the yard and the piles of garbage.

"More flies?" Ms. McKreutzer asked nervously.

"No," Elliot said. "Ants."

"My goodness," Ms. McKreutzer said. "Are they, ah, *inside* the house, too?"

Elliot nodded. "Yes," he said. "We—"

"I know. You like it that way," Ms. McKreutzer said.

One day Elliot didn't come to school. *Absent*, Ms. McKreutzer wrote in her book after Elliot's name.

The next day she wrote *Absent* again.

School was a little boring without Elliot there. The children wished he would come back so that they could see what he would add to his picture.

With an orange crayon Elizabeth added some new blossoms to the zinnias in her yard. "Nice," the other children said.

Alvinia used her set of deluxe acrylic paints and carefully painted pink hair ribbons on her three poodles. "Cute," Ms. McKreutzer said. She yawned a little bit, politely holding her hand in front of her mouth.

Everyone looked at the picture of Elliot's house and wished that Elliot would return.

"Ms. McKreutzer," one of the children said suddenly, looking very surprised, "there's no house left!"

It was true. They all stared at the picture and realized that it was true. Elliot's house had disappeared behind the mounds of garbage and trash. They could see a tiny chunk of chimney sticking out from behind a mountain of dirty laundry that had been tossed onto the roof. But that was the only thing left of the original house that Elliot had drawn.

"My goodness, class," Ms. McKreutzer said. "I think we should investigate this."

The entire class peered from the windows of the school bus that took them on their search. Ms. McKreutzer had Elliot's address written on an index card. She read it to the school-bus driver fourteen times as he drove around the block again and again.

Finally he stopped the bus. He sighed. He was a little annoyed because he had won first prize in navigation at bus driver's school. Never before had he failed to find an address.

"It should have been right here," he said in a peevish voice, "but it isn't." He pointed to a field between two houses.

The children stared. It was a messy vacant lot with some vehicles in it. A steam shovel was scooping dirt from one place and depositing it in another. A Caterpillar tractor was smoothing the mounds. A ragged corner of a pizza box fluttered in the breeze. Then it disappeared under a shovelful of dirt.

There was a sign tacked to the fence. The children read the sign together.

"*Landfill*," they all read aloud.

"*Landfill* is a compound word, class," Ms. Mc-Kreutzer pointed out. She was a teacher, after all.

"*Elliot* is landfill," the class replied. "He likes it that way," they added.

They missed him. But after a while he was only a dim memory. When his picture, hanging on the classroom wall, became faded and curled at the edges, someone took it down and threw it away. It was recycled.

Jellies

•

BY *Ruth Heller*

Like ice cream on a summer day
jellyfish will melt away
as the sun grows hot and hotter
if they're stranded out of water.

These fascinating blobs of gel
have no bones and have no shell.
They pulsate as they jet propel,
or at the mercy of the tide,
hitch a ride.

Let's have healthy, wholesome seas
for living treasures such as these
translucent purple, milky blue
jellies you can see right through.
Some are so clear they disappear,
but like a crystal chandelier,
they more or less . . .

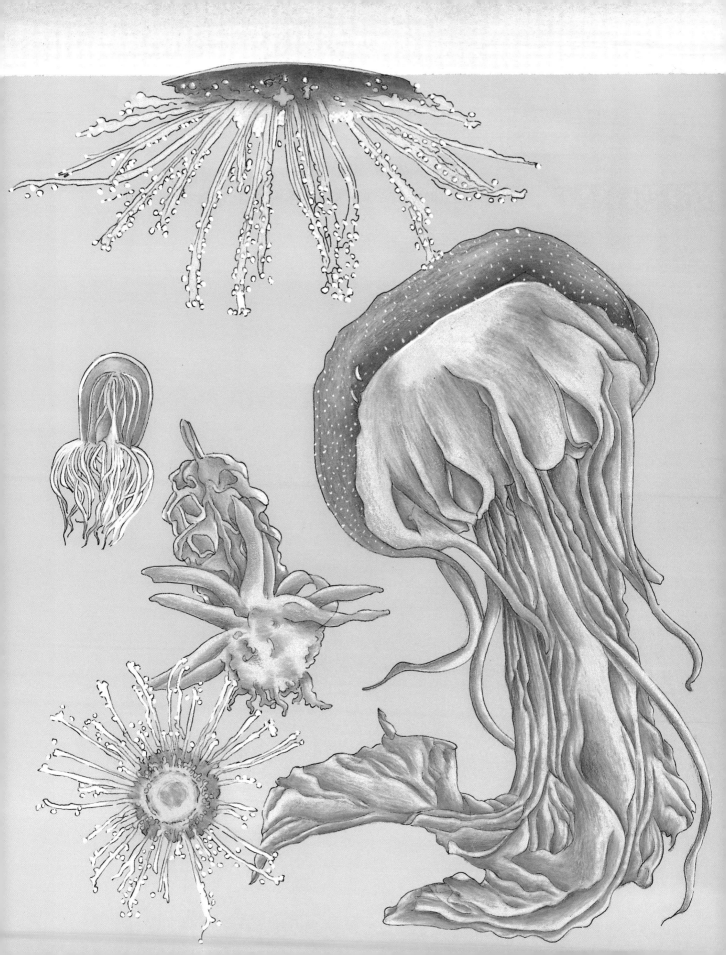

. . . fluoresce.

Let's have no spills of oily fuels
to hinder all these jelly jewels
that light up in the deep.
But do not touch or you may weep,
because those fragile trailing things
are tentacles with nasty stings.

Small fish are very much surprised,
because they never realized
that they'd be stunned and paralyzed
to satisfy the hungry wishes
of voracious jellyfishes.

Bringing the Prairie Home

•

BY *Patricia MacLachlan*

•

ILLUSTRATED BY *Steve Johnson*
AND *Lou Fancher*

Place.

This is one of my favorite words, and I am a writer because of it.

Place.

I remember vividly the place where I was born: the smell of the earth, the look of the skies when storms came through; the softness of my mother's hollyhock blooms that grew by the back fence.

When I was ten years old, I fell in love with place. My parents and I drove through the prairie, great stretches of land between small towns named wonderful names like Spotted Horse, Rattlesnake, Sunrise. We stopped once for drinks that we fished out of cold-water lift-top tanks, and my mother and I walked out onto the prairie. Then my mother said something that changed my life forever. She took a step, looked down at her footprint, and said, "Someone long ago may have walked here, or maybe no one ever has. Either way it's history."

I thought of those who might have come before me and those who might come after, but mostly I was face-to-face with the important, hopeful permanence of place, place that I knew was there long before I walked there, and would be there long after I was gone. I realized, in that moment, that the Earth is history. The Earth is like a character who has secrets; the Earth holds important clues to who we are, who we've been; who we will be. We are connected to the land and to those secrets.

It was after this event that I bought a diary and began writing all sorts of truths about myself, as if I, too, might leave clues about myself behind. I was becoming a writer. All because of place. Now I cannot write a story unless I know the place, the landscape that shapes the story and

the people in the story. And to remind myself of the place that changed me, I have carried a small bag of prairie dirt with me for years.

I took that bag of prairie dirt with me once to a class of fourth graders, and I found that those children are connected to place, too. Some had moved from place to place many times: One boy's house had burned in a fire recently; another was about to move to a place he had never been.

"Maybe," I said, "I should toss this out onto my New England yard. I'll probably never live on the prairie again."

"*No!*" cried a boy, horrified. "It might blow away!"

And then a girl had a suggestion.

"Maybe you should put that prairie dirt in a glass on your windowsill, so you can see it when you write. It would be like bringing the prairie home."

And that is where that little piece of my prairie is today; my place, my past, my landscape; in a glass on my windowsill. I have brought the prairie home so that I can look at it every day; write about it, write about me, and remind myself that the land is the connection that links us all.

A SONG FOR FRANCIS OF ASSISI:
PATRON OF ECOLOGY

BY TOMIE dePAOLA

O, LITTLE MAN
IN YOUR TATTERED ROBE,
HOW DID YOU KNOW
SO MUCH?
HOW DID YOU KNOW
THAT ALL THINGS,
ALL BEINGS,
ALL BIRDS,

ALL ANIMALS,
ALL CREATURES OF EACH RIVER,
EACH SEA,
ALL OLIVE TREES,
ALL FLOWERS,
ALL BLADES OF GRASS,
FIRE, WATER,

SUN AND MOON AND STARS,
ARE ALL GOD'S CREATIONS;
AND TO LOVE GOD,
WE MUST LOVE ALL THE UNIVERSE;
EACH FOREST,
EACH DROP OF PURE WATER,
EACH BREATH OF FRESH AIR,
ALL THINGS, WE MUST CARE FOR.

O, LITTLE MAN
IN YOUR TATTERED ROBE,
REMIND US AGAIN,
WHAT YOU KNEW,
REMIND US
GENTLY, FIRMLY.

ORA PRO NOBIS.

Dear Earth

•

BY *Karla Kuskin*

•

ILLUSTRATED BY *Jerry Pinkney*

I'm sitting on an old, cold star,
me and a lot of stones.
Not a tree or a bird
or a chair.
I'm looking out across an endless curve of sky
across an empty universe of air
to where my world spins
tree green, sea blue,
there.
City, windows, house and room,
crayons, bike, bed, book and bear
there.
Snug
and VERY
far
far
far
away.

Dear Earth
I miss your green and blue.
I miss my room and bear.
It's dull and lonely here on this old star.
I miss your night, Dear Earth,
the moon above, the cool dark grass below.
I miss each always-different, ever-changing day.
You know the way you are, Dear Earth.
Well, stay that way.

The contributors' royalties and proceeds from the publisher's sale of the book will be donated to the following organizations to further their work for our planet:

The Children's Rainforest USA, linked to sister organizations in other countries, was established to promote awareness of and education about rain forests. The organization also channels, through the Monteverde Conservation League, all monetary contributions in their entirety to preserve undisturbed tropical rain forests in Costa Rica. To learn more, write to: The Children's Rainforest, P.O. Box 936, Lewiston, ME 04240.

Conservation International identifies places where the Earth's richest diversity of plant and animal species can be found, creating conservation solutions through innovative, people-centered programs that are economically sound and scientifically based. To learn more, write to: Conservation International, 1015 Eighteenth Street NW, Suite 1000, Washington, DC 20036.

Through 600,000 active members, numerous publications, and education programs in classrooms and nature sanctuaries, the **National Audubon Society** is committed both to fostering respect for the natural world among children and adults and to encouraging individual participation in issues affecting wildlife habitat. To learn more, write to: National Audubon Society, 700 Broadway, New York, NY 10003 (phone 212-979-3000).

The **Natural Resources Defense Council** (NRDC) uses the power of law, science, and people to safeguard our planet. NRDC defends America's magnificent forests, rivers, coasts, and wildlife against exploitation and destruction. Internationally, NRDC is leading efforts to save the ozone layer, protect rain forests, and reverse global warming. To learn more, write to: Membership Department, NRDC, 40 West Twentieth Street, New York, NY 10011 (phone 212-727-2700).

The Nature Conservancy is an international conservation organization committed to preserving plants, animals, and natural communities that represent the diversity of life on Earth by protecting the land and water they need to survive. The conservancy owns and manages the largest privately owned nature preserve system in the world. To learn more, write to: The Nature Conservancy, 1815 North Lynn Street, Arlington, VA 22209.

For nearly a century, the field staff of **NYZS The Wildlife Conservation Society** (WCS) has studied wildlife species, established parks and reserves, trained wildlife experts, and taught people about conservation. Known in forty-four countries as "the muddy boots organization," WCS depends upon familiarity with local conditions and ecology to effect realistic conservation action and policy. To learn more, write to: NYZS The Wildlife Conservation Society, Bronx, NY 10460 (phone 718-220-6891).